Weather Watchers

Rain

Cassie Mayer

Heinemann Library
Chicago, Illinois

Customer Service   888–454–2279

Visit our website at www.heinemannlibrary.com

Photo research by Tracy Cummins, Tracey Engel, and Ruth Blair
Designed by Jo Hinton-Malivoire
Printed and bound in China by South China Printing Company

10 09 08 07 06
10 9 8 7 6 5 4 3 2 1

Library of Congress Cataloging-in-Publication Data
Mayer, Cassie.
  Rain / Cassie Mayer.
    p. cm. -- (Weather watchers)
  Includes bibliographical references and index.
  ISBN-13: 978-1-4034-8414-7 (library binding-hardcover : alk. paper)
  ISBN-10: 1-4034-8414-7 (library binding-hardcover : alk. paper)
  ISBN-13: 978-1-4034-8422-2 (pbk. : alk. paper)
  ISBN 1-4034-8422-8 (pbk. : alk. paper)
  1. Rain and rainfall--Juvenile literature. I. Title. II. Series.
  QC924.7.M39 2007
  551.57'7--dc22

                        2006007904

Acknowledgments
The author and publisher are grateful to the following for permission to reproduce copyright material:
Corbis pp. **4** (cloud; sunshine, G. Schuster/zefa), **5** (Anthony Redpath), **14** (Royalty Free), **15** (Bruce Peebles), **18** (ARKO DATTA/Reuters), **21** (Simon Marcus); Getty Images pp. **4** (lightning; snow, Marc Wilson Photography), **6** (George Grall), **16** (Jeremy Woodhouse), **17** (altrendo nature), **19** (David Woodfall), **20** (Steve Satushek), **23** (cracked clay, altrendo nature; flood David Woodfall).

Cover photograph reproduced with permission of Corbis (Anthony Redpath).
Back cover photograph reproduced with permission of Corbis (ARKO DATTA/Reuters).

Every effort has been made to contact copyright holders of any material reproduced in this book.
Any omissions will be rectified in subsequent printings if notice is given to the publisher.

Contents

What Is Weather?

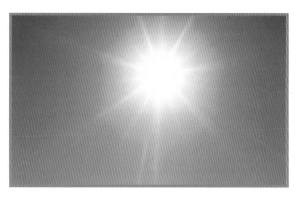

Weather is what the air is like outside.
Weather can change all the time.

Rain is a type of weather.

What Is Rain?

Rain is water that falls from clouds.

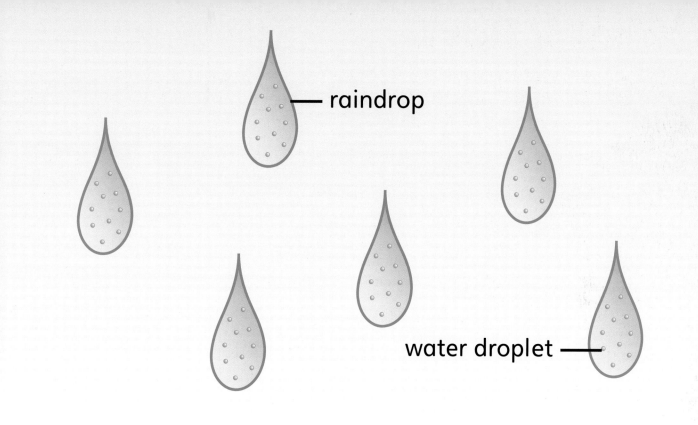

raindrop

water droplet

Raindrops are made from tiny drops of water. These are called water droplets.

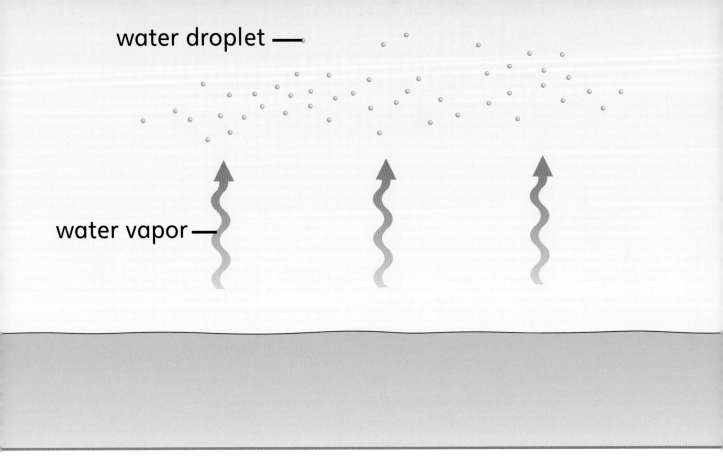

water droplet —

water vapor —

Water droplets are made from water vapor.

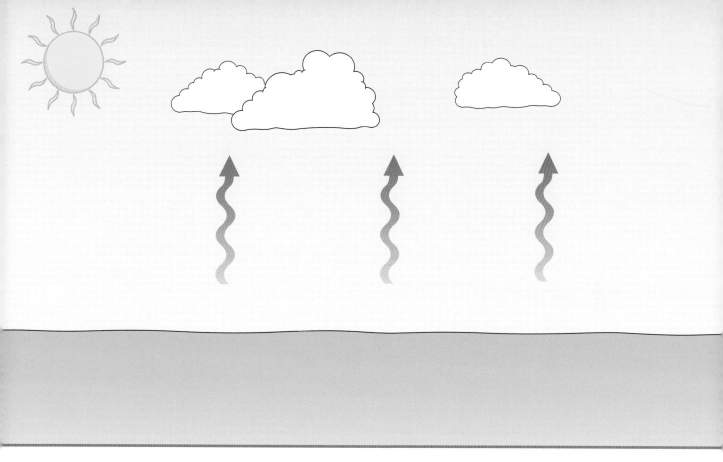

Water vapor is part of the air outside.

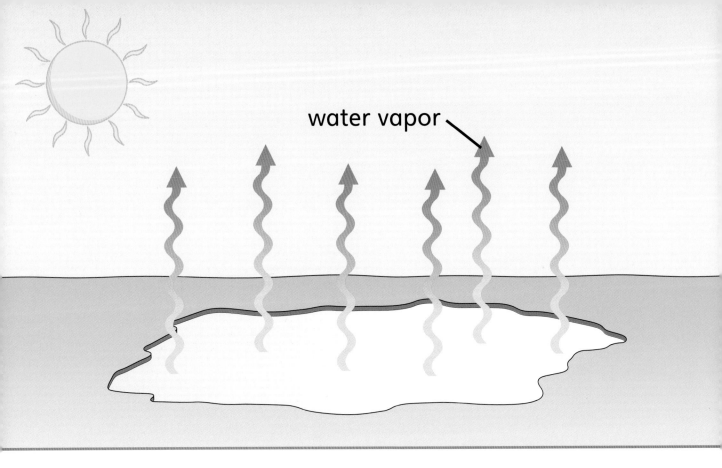

water vapor

Water vapor comes from oceans.
Water vapor comes from lakes.

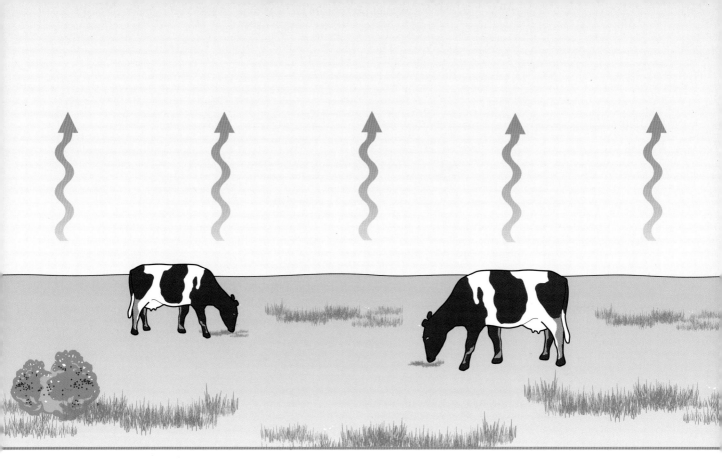

Water vapor comes from plants.
Water vapor comes from animals.

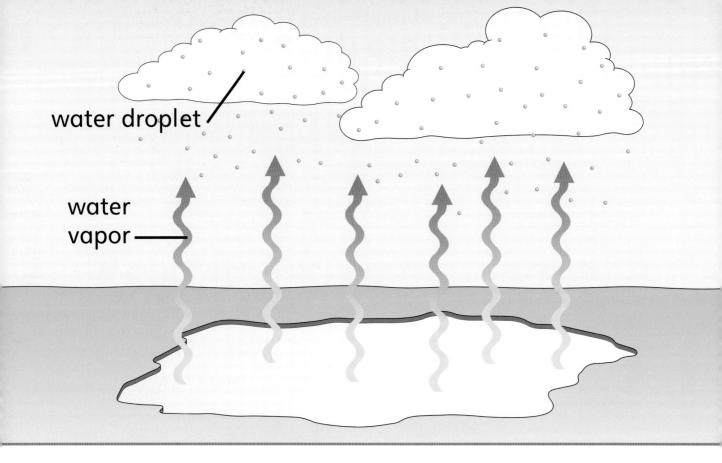

water droplet

water vapor

Water vapor rises into the air.
Water vapor forms water droplets.

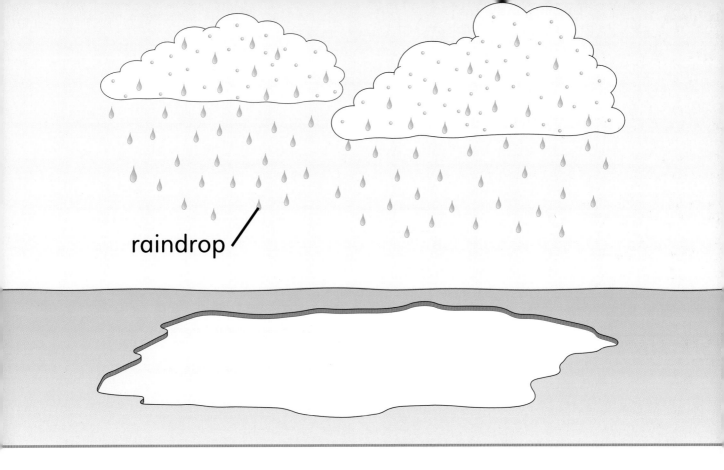

raindrop

Water droplets form raindrops.
Raindrops fall from clouds.

Types of Rain

Sometimes it rains a little.

Sometimes it rains a lot.

Sometimes it does not rain for a long time. There is not enough water.

This is called a drought.

Sometimes it rains too much.
There is too much water.

This is called a flood.

How Does Rain Help Us?

All living things need water.
Rain brings water back to the earth.

Rain is an important part of our weather. Rain can also be fun!

What to Wear in the Rain

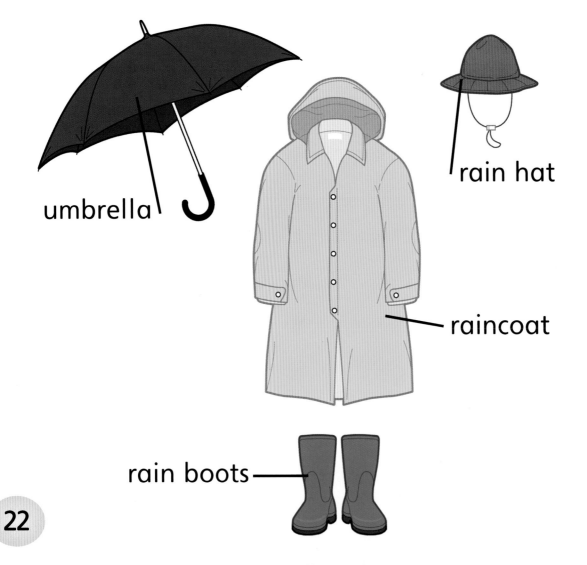

umbrella

rain hat

raincoat

rain boots

Picture Glossary

drought when it does not rain for a long time

flood when there is too much water on the land

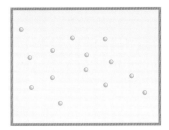

water droplet a tiny drop of water. Water droplets are smaller than raindrops.

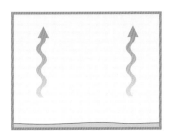

water vapor part of the air outside

Index

Note to Parents and Teachers
This series introduces children to the concept of weather and its importance in our lives. Discuss with children the types of weather that they are already familiar with, and point out how weather changes season by season.

In this book, children explore rain. Diagrams are included to enhance students' understanding of how rain is formed. The text has been chosen with the advice of a literacy expert to enable beginning readers success reading independently or with moderate support. An expert in the field of meteorology was consulted to ensure accurate content. You can support children's nonfiction literacy skills by helping them use the table of contents, headings, picture glossary, and index.